SEEDS

# S E E D S

Poetry

Emilie K. Hill

"to be left open

with see-through glass"

To Luke Hill,

for helping me come alive.

# CONTENTS

# CONTENTS

# CONTENTS

# AKNOWLEDGMENTS

Thank you to my husband and family who has
encouraged me to put my words on paper for
others to know. Thank you Lynette Bowhay,
for showing me how much of a gift life is
and those we spend it with.

A special thanks to Erika Cimino, who
helped this dream become a reality with
her artwork and design for the book cover.

# A  SEED

A seed sat quietly

surrounded by those she loved

Waiting, they poured into her

and hoped with dedication

for growth


But she needed more time

the darkness was comfortable

because it was all she knew

She could feel the anticipation

around her

the pull that asked her to move forward


We had pictures in our mind

of what she would look like

and we imagined her thick leaves

with beautiful glow

all the details

that would make us wonder

but she saw nothing

all she could do was feel

and remember what was keeping her there


However, she knew she didn't want this

as her forever

so she took a deep breath

and joined us in the waiting


Together we squirmed

and little changes began

It looked like not much was happening

until her roots grew sturdier

and she stood there tall

"Look!" we cried

and our tears fell into her soil

giving her the nourishment she lacked


With heavy hearts

we knew the wait was worth it

Our hope was not in vain

Only the few who stood by

could witness a moment

so complete

# ENGLAND

I hear the sound of my boots

follow me home

as they walk upon the cobblestone roads

that know secrets from

years beyond my life


Inside, I am greeted by instant warmth

from the fire

and the sound of laughter

from the other students

that fills the room


The window floods with fog

as I press my nose

against the cold glass

I watch the pedestrians

cross the streets

in a hurry

wondering if they cherish this place

like I do


I dread my return to California

to a place where rain is a visitor

and tea is drank occasionally

so I hug mine closer between my hands

and listen to the new sounds

that I've come to know well


on this fall afternoon

in York


Right now it is routine

but I know how

I will long for it later

# DECISIONS

I let myself feel

what I want to feel

but argue with all there is to say

Where to go from here

someone needs to decide

while I choose to hide

behind the mistakes of the future


I chose to make no decisions at all

which is where I messed up most


Because hiding from a life

of possibilities

is the worst decision of all

# WILLOWS

Where the willows weep

songs are sung


Where sorrow is known

healing has begun

LDB

More often than not

I question why you left

why you had to go

and why you couldn't stay

I beg you to return

and plea for forgiveness

wishing there was something I could do


I reflect on what has already happened

and what could have been

but each and every time

I am reminded again


You saw a life none of us had to see

You had to love while running on empty

You truly tried to seek for the beauty

in this life

but reality crept up

and you couldn't help but sink


You cried for help

and even jumped overboard

but you could only swim so far

without realizing

the anchor would only pull you back

to your worst memories


If only you never tasted a life

so sweet

and disaster may have not won

but to live in fear

and endlessly run with no fresh air to

gasp,

how could anyone last?


I want you to try once more

and sail another sea

but we are bonded to the ships

we were given

and the storms blind what more

we could be


So the next time I ask you

to be here

with me

I'll think of the life you once had

and the fact that you

are now free

## SPOTLIGHT

I walk upon the stage

all eyes on me


In this spotlight

they feel sympathy

and see my shame

the things I should change


Let me bring you to the shadows

where my name meets you first

before the lies

we believe too well


Despair hides the parts

that long for display

Give them a chance

and I will too

then perhaps

they can finally

break through

# ESCAPE

Every flower has its flaw

even those that try not

to be picked at all

So then what happens

when one chooses to be alone

and it has nothing more to atone?


There is a chance it may escape

but only a few never break


The plan may blossom beautifully

but the thunder and its storm

and the rain

that does nothing but mourn

shatters what could have been

when something so fragile

continues to chase the hopeless wind

# HUMAN

It's either love or rejection

that wins

either a heart full of care

or selfishness

whatever makes it easiest

to just be

But what we all really long for

are the things

we are most afraid of giving

If we all hide behind what we can offer

what is the point in being

at all?

# THE JAR

But if things could be any different
and the scratches would eventually fade
I would not have chosen
to be left open
with see-through glass
and so delicately made

My green appearance
and useful ways
make me a desirable appliance
for as long as I stay

Things enter me and leave me
according to their need
and time and time again

I make people bleed


Its not much use to be pretty at all

when no one can determine

the fall

The noise is quite loud

and it can make a scene

but no one understands

what its like for me


"We can fix it," they say

but how much use

can a jar really be

when it can no longer hold

and do as it is told


The broken pieces make it

easier to let go

because after all

its not too hard to get ahold

of another who looks just like me


I was carried off as I watched

my replacement

and admired her beauty


I wondered what more

she could give them

than I ever could

as my once excited owner

threw me out for good

# WITHOUT YOU

I wished

I could simply say,

"we will laugh once again",

as our hearts taught us how to do


But how can I look into your eyes

of hate

and repeat the whispered words

of such a fate


I loved you the best I knew

Show me your love was love

so I can continue

without you

## WOMAN

I marveled at her beauty

Thick curls resting on her soft skin

hiding her neck

that only she knew well


Her breasts were full

but I kept my eyes

away from them

to admire what they framed


Her cheekbones were confident

and spoke of the depth within

Her lips youthful,

with promise of sincerity

Her legs were thick

strong and graceful

I caught glimpses of the painter

capturing her image carefully

but was too distracted

by the real thing


I watched her nervously adjust her head

to find comfort in being watched

so closely

and wished she could understand

what I saw

not what she imagined to be


The painter cleaned his tools

decisively finished with his work

and I froze

Before me was not the image I had seen

with my very own eyes -

the woman with so much

intriguing beauty

that I just studied


It was an ordinary picture

of a woman with boney legs

not much different than my own

with boring breasts

and much more of proud look

than I witnessed


"This painter must be corrected,"

I thought

but no words came to my lips

And to this day

I think of this woman

and wish she could see herself

as she was

and not what he thought

she should be

## SEARCHING

If moonlight was enough to show you

I'd rest knowing

my lips could be


After hours my voice is hoarse

and my cheeks burn from confusion

My mind wanders

but my words won't follow


If the chaos could somehow listen

I could explain

I know you're searching

you might find me there

# BUT

Authenticity is always right there,

waiting,

giving a way out

back home


She has so much joy there,

abounding amity,

But distortion

drew her in

BEST THINGS

Juvenile and daunted
I let it come close
and tell me where to flea

Promises felt distant
and unlikely to be
so the borrowed dress, and
words that eased the pain,
gave me hope to look beyond
the towering gloom and rain

I could feel it on my skin
some days colder
others almost numb

But the best things in front of me,
said they were good enough


I believed the darkness
that it would show me the way
It felt a lot brighter
than being alone
"So for now," I would say,
"this is my home."


But darkness feels so much darker,
in the presence of light


My hands trembled in the shining words
it spoke
yet I could feel the fog upon me
like a big, dark cloak

It told me why I am safe

right where I'm at


This time, I didn't believe it

How could I


when the best things

that had kept me there

were now visible,

lies

## WHERE WE ARE HEADED

Overcast reminds me of tender days

when we let our fascination

have its way


Blocked roads

and blurry vision

gave an explanation

of where reverence

ends all too soon


My voice quivers

as this old snow lingers,

is there any warmth

left for us?

Backward or onward,

one of us has to know

where we are headed


before it all is too clear to see

I am continuing this way,

wherever that may be

# HUME

When my feelings are vocalized

they feel dry and expected

repeated and misunderstood

but in my mind

they are powerful and

known


I keep the unspoken thoughts to myself

to cherish and perfect

hoping they can find a way out

on their own


Then there's the pull of the trees

the summer air in the mountains

that feels thick and piercing

yet wholesome and comforting

Many days have been spent in this place
of refuge
where wandering thoughts
could find rest
where I am reminded
what I was created for

I need to express
these magnificent pictures
of strength and beauty
shared by the chirping in the distance
and the quietness of nature's language
that only your soul can hear

The ordinary

looking so new and inviting

to celebrate


but out loud these secrets

and whispers from God

sound empty and tried

so I put them aside

to enjoy another day

when they are ready to speak

# FUTURE

Eternal grace

seeps past the image of

your face

when memories speak louder

than words


I hear your old whispers

of the future

but am left with pictures

of your noose


How did you end up there,

and me here?

## MOTHER'S SINS

You dressed yourself in roses

when your body

called out for water

You knelt before the podium

at the feet of your mother's sins

There was only so much you could do

with hardly anything

left to give

I watched as they carried you away

nothing but dust

while she fell to the floor

begging for something

she stole

## YOU

Cover to cover

you've known all along

Yet weeks, chapters, years,

I carried on


Lost opportunities

and extra affliction

remind me of you

cause now all I can see

is a story of pursuit

and a battle

you already won

## DAYLIGHT

Daylight

you come and go

sometimes I think

I'll never know

when you'll return


But the next morning

just as you promised

my tears have dried

and a new day

is upon me

## QUIET PRESENCE

If only you could see

what once was here

and what it's become


There's a reason the pain

no longer wins

and my hope

no longer sways


When everything is different

than it seemed

and the promises you trusted

vanish

what is left?

I could not comfort myself

when I deceived myself so cruelly

and I could not explain to others

what I hardly could explain to me


But the quiet presence that said

nothing at all

was everything I needed


It spoke louder than the words

that were too often heard

and softened my heart

when everything else hurt

# SOUL STRINGS

There is something

about gloom

that puts my heart in tune


The tapping of the tears

falling from the sky

rejoicing

as they fly


It is then when a book naturally opens

in my hand

connecting me

with who I am


Pleasure is found in savoring

berries handpicked

from a field

they cannot compare to the ones

carefully cleaned and sealed


The thought of green pastures

in cold climates

far away from my own

tears into any contentment

I may have known


If there was a way to always live

with such wonderful things,

joy would constantly be pulling

my soul strings


Perhaps I can linger

on the feelings these treasures bring

or find their resemblance

in almost anything

JUNK

Who filled my bath

with all this junk

It wasn't me,

it wasn't the maid.

Not the dog,

nor the cat.

If it wasn't them,

and wasn't me,

who is to blame?

Then, I knew

it spoke on its own

as shame is the loudest

and fills the room

from head to toe,

wall crevice to crevice,

junk claimed my home

## DIFFERENT

Staring into this mirror

gives me doubt

that I could look into the window

and see something different


The pearls around my neck

remind me of sweet words said to me

long ago


I savor them

to bandage my leaking heart

that wants to burst

"Don't be this way",

I tell myself

I catch a breath

as my corset squeezes my flaws

the party downstairs awaits,

so I head for the door

I have a lot to offer

can they tell?


As long as no one can see

my smeared mascara

and shaking hands,


they can

## THE FINAL SAY

Dawn to dusk

I wait for you


My mind falls short of

accuracy

My answers need

revision


My voice as the final say means:

goodbye, good day

a smile with closed lips

mistakes memorized

and chosen emotion


I close my eyes to wait for your

arrival

to hear

what you see

YOUR SHOW

Mixed messages

led me here

a place where I have duties

to be what I should for those around

yet am stuck

in need of them too


Too much

Too little

I cannot tell

so continue to guide me

where I should grow


I was vocal and hungry

but soon hushed

so I became supple and diffident

leaving them eager to know


Relying on your direction

left me with a conflict

leading to destruction


But because of what I was taught most

you'll never see it

just an answer

and a show

# HOME

A quiet home

filled with people

can feel more

lively

than a house full

of voices, laughter,

and stories

One looks reality in the face

and the other hides loneliness

behind a smile

## REMINDER

The inexpressible joy

that comes in a moment

can never warn you

of the anger of tomorrow


Grief may swallow you

and never let go

until you

choose to look beyond

what is in front of you


Wherever you dwell

there is a reason to

mourn

a reason to question

any beauty you ever knew


But without the reminder

of cherished times

and conquered hardships

you could miss out

on things right under your nose


Notice others who are hurting

and need to know it is okay

It will and can be

if it is done together

and not in the shadows of loss


In every small thing

there is a glimpse of purpose,

of something beautiful to come

Don't miss it

cause it won't make itself known

if you aren't looking

## TWO-TONED

Glory hides

behind the shadow of your confidence

they marvel at what they see

and whisper about what they don't


But everything is two-toned

like the magnolia leaves

framing your home


The green on the front

invites you in to see

while the brown on the inside remains

a harmonious secret


The yellows and pinks on my garden

flowers

steal the show

but all I feel is black and blue

the side you're not used to

## FEELINGS

How can I feel

so happy and so sad

at the same time


Both feelings compete to win

and moment to moment

I give them their time


It'd be best if one could stay

but they have me confused

coming and going so quickly,

I don't know which one to listen to


They both stand up

with such strong points

but neither one will finish

or stay long enough

to prove their point

Every time,

they almost have me

and then it switches

and all contradicts


So tell me,

one of you,

"am I to be happy or sad"?


They both speak at once

and say,

"Happy"

"Sad"

THE WIND

The wind

pushes and pulls

as she passionately protests


If you listen carefully

without your

orchestrated thoughts

you might join

## L D H

Your voice echoes

deep into my ears

repeating the words

that has haunted me for years


We are very alike

in many ways

the main reason

we could talk endlessly

for days


The words that tell you

you will never be enough

are the same that made me think

I could never love

But do you see us now

my darling one

we are living proof

there's no too great of damage

we could have done


I will help you see

as you will for me

however ugly

life may be


Together we are three;

Jesus

you

me

where there is

victory

Changes blind our goal

leaving us scarred

and forgetful


But we always

start new

when we refuse the lies

to remember our potential

# ANXIETY

Searching a face

while seeing your own

while trying to be present


While wrestling with your words

and thoughts

as they find their way out

when you already regretted them

before they did


While hiding behind

true answers

to say whatever

feels safest

While shuffling through identities

to find the one

you think they'd want you to posses

While they try to get to know you

when you can't even get to

know yourself

when you can't even remember

who you should be

or where you're wrong

or where they are right

This is anxiety.

## BEDROOM DOOR

My bedroom door

kept me from getting the help

I needed most

But the times I left it open

remind me

of how little of a difference

it made

At least when it was closed

I could pretend

I had another option

# UNDERNEATH

Underneath the sandy cove

lies slanted, undiscovered rock

that restricts the tide


The line left on the sand from

the water

defines

where it has touched

and where it remains dry


I watch and wait

wishing for it to come closer

to feel the cold water

bring relief from the heat

I dig my toes in deeper

until the grainy bits resist my feet


The warmth from the wind pursues me

and I'm held there

securely

letting the salty air

wrap all around me


Unaware that I was digging further,

distracted by the love

that I used to fear,

sudden pain grabbed the inside

of my foot


I broke the hold

and lifted my leg to see

blood trickling across

the callused skin


And that is when I discovered

the rock,

underneath

MORE

Its settle

but its here

When noise and anguish

almost drown it out

there are glimpses of

something more


In between the static

and what seems to be so clear

is the truth we all long for

but protect ourselves from


Disappointment is seen

on a young mans face

the same rejection he felt

for the first time

from his father

but deep down

if he only knew

there is things only he

could bring to the world


A mother cries over her lifeless child

afraid to carry this unforeseen weight

on her own


But joy

can be found in the oceans character

in the innocence of a smile

or the silence and gracefulness of the

mysterious moon

There is more

we just have to look for it


We were created to feel it

know it


But confusion feels easier

and more powerful

than the steady truth

that can heal your soul

CAVITIES


Cavities

from the things I've swallowed

don't let me forget them

in every new bite I take


I miss the days of enjoying

something sweet

without enduring aches


Is it mistakes I have made

or something that comes with life


If I tell you

of the things I feel

I fear I will continue to go on alone

and have to bring dismissal,

defeat, & dander

to only name a few


The dentist

helped me numb the wounds

but I can already feel it

seeping through

reminding me that

they are coming too

EJH

I squeeze you tighter

and kiss the nose

I gave you

as I remember when your tiny body

melted against me

for the very first time


I long to step

into that memory

and memorize

every detail


when our fragile bones

and timid eyes

locked

painful hours of the night

I was in shock

that I could keep you

that your body came from mine

It was the start of new lives

with new names and

world around us

to figure out

together

# THE CHURCH

The church

is old and worn

large and dusty

From the back pews

are whispers of fear and regret


Only those listening can hear them

but most of us are busy pretending


We desire the freedom

we often discuss

but hide behind an "amen"

to receive an undeserved "well done"


Some come out strong and wise

but others, like me

quit

before they are told they won't make it


Yet God's presence is undeniable

and holds my hand

as I watch the preacher speak

opposite of what

he does


If it was not for Jesus,

my only constant friend and

Father

my whispers, like many others,

would have quieted

and would long for rest elsewhere

But behind the preacher I see the cross

and am reminded

of where we all fall short

So I respond to the whispers

and tears behind me and say,

"me too"

## ALLEYWAYS

Every hour

I check the clock

waiting for the moment

That I can stop


The memories flood my mind

of a time

I took wrong turns

and pretended I meant

to swerve


But in the alleyways

I let go of you

and cry before you return

I can't catch up

so don't ask me to


but deep down

I know

It's me who is begging you

## A DREAM


This friend of mine

is kind

but recently has become more reserved,

distant

which makes me question where we stand


I remembered times he was nice

and as I listened to him speak,

his voice slowly became deeper

saying,

"don't be offended

but

the choices you are making..."


The words repeated but I noticed it was

no longer his voice

but another man's

who was much older and serious

saying, "Don't be offended

but

the choices you are making..."


This time I heard it

over a loud speaker

and found

myself watching a dark

steam engine train

slowly creeping past

my view


The pilot was painted

with black and white stripes

resembling a prisoner

There were many skinny corpses

in worn out,

ripped clothing

lying still and cold

in the evening winter night

side by side on each passing

flat railroad car

I saw my breath in the crisp air

and was overcome with guilt

## PRAISE

Ugly has power

not one wants to admit

Yet we speak of it as though

it is only a myth


Regardless of praised

beauty

both hidden and seen

We can all be found guilty

of not knowing what

it means

AGAIN

I went for a walk

to quiet the noise

and sirens came my way

as it carried a person

to their end


I flipped on the T.V.

to find some distraction

but the newscasters

yelled at me

as if I could make a difference


My telephone rang

but I refused to answer it

doubting there was much to say

I opened a book

to learn of other lives

but could too easily

predict the ending


so I went to bed

and woke up to a screaming alarm clock

to do it all over again

# TIME

Its half past seven

and I can still feel

the sunshine on my skin


I can hear your voice

an hour after you left

and closed the door behind you


From years ago

I can taste the food you made

and want more


How long before I stop missing you?


Because it still feels

like just seconds ago

your toes touched the same sand

before

I was only minutes too late


If time won't tell,

than what will?

# RUTHLESS

Enraptured by the fury

that comes with the wind

I gather thoughts

that try to remain unconscious


Speak the wisdom

you've come to know

or let it forever

conspire

into foolish pits

you've let go


Yesterday's shadows

are ruthless

and hide not

today's worries

My senses tell

otherwise

in fear of regret


And suddenly

the sun shines

differently

as if

it had never been

# THANK YOU

Give grace to the humble
and tear down these walls
The story within me
needs you most of all


in the name of my Father
in the name of His Son
Bring healing to this heart
and what is to come


I thank you for
what you've already begun
with hope in the mystery
it will be done

DRD

She started off

with endless opportunities

and a mind of her own

a heart for you and me

and the strange men in her home


she had plans

to be something special

but was handed a match

at only age five

her world burned around her

before she was old enough

to tell anyone about it


From the beginning

she survived in ruins

the smell of drugs on her mother

was comfort she was still nearby

she looked after her siblings

like the mother

she longed for


I met her years later

when she was flying over that place

she never wanted to land

I watched in awe

that someone could be so brave

and never look back


but her new story

became much like her old one

where things repeat

and are broken

no matter how far she gets

she is met

by a match

disguised in sheep's clothing

and is forced to watch

anything that is left

burn

Yet,

through the flames

I see the girl

with endless opportunities

with a mind of her own

in memories

that could not have been

if she had not


She pushes me forward

as we step on thorns

together

until I look to see

that my feet are safe

and she has gone back

to where it all started

Throughout our life, we are given many

s e e d s.


It is up to us what we do with them and

whether or not they have the chance to

grow into something beautiful.

# ABOUT THE AUTHOR

Emilie K. Hill is a wife, mother and friend to many who have inspired her to share her thoughts with the world. She speaks boldly about the depression, anxiety, and fear that lurks in the corner of our hearts. Her first book of poetry "Seeds" is meant to inspire anyone to find light in the dark world we live in.

37766873R00068

Made in the USA
Middletown, DE
05 March 2019